Hidden Friends

Growing in Prayer

Carmelites
of Indianapolis

Sheed & Ward
Kansas City

Sheed & Ward™ is a service of The National Catholic Reporter
Publishing Company.

ISBN: 1-55612-824-X

Published by: Sheed & Ward
                115 E. Armour Blvd.
                P.O. Box 419492
                Kansas City, MO 64141-6492

Cover design by Emil Antonucci.

To order, call: (800) 333-7373

Contents

Dedication

To Sr. Miriam Elder, OCD (1907–1995) whose wisdom, love for God and fidelity to prayer has shaped the life of our community.

Foreword

Spirituality becomes real as our relationship with the Divine shapes our choices, attitudes, self-image, world view and relationships. In Carmel we live with the articulated spirituality of our Saints, seeing more deeply into our every day experience in the light of theirs. This book of art and reflection is the fruit of this process. It comes from our inner world and is offered to yours.

Jean Alice McGoff, OCD
Prioress, Carmelite Monastery
Indianapolis, Indiana

Contributors:
Teresa M. Boersig, OCD
Ruth Ann Boyle, OCD
Rosemary Crump, OCD
Joanne Dewald, OCD
Selena Kilmoyer, OCD
Elizabeth Meluch, OCD

Artist: Selena Kilmoyer, OCD

Acknowledgments

There are a number of friends who have been particularly helpful in reviewing the art work and reflections and giving us valuable suggestions. One reader mentioned it allowed her to experience "sacred moments." We wish to thank Rev. Larry Voelker, pastor of Holy Name Parish, Beech Grove, Indiana, Rev. Susan N. Deverall, S.T.M., Minister of Lizton Christian Church (Disciples of Christ), Rev. Andrea Hughes Leininger, M.Div., Pastor, Calvary United Methodist Church, Brownsburg, Indiana, Rev. Sue Reid, M.Div., S.M.M., Episcopal Diocese of Indianapolis, Mary K. Cove, Ph.D., Mary Jo Matheny, Mary Catherine Gibson and Sr. Margaret Kelly.

Our gratitude to Pat Stevens for encouraging us to undertake this project and her contribution to the writing. Elaine Theisen OCDS, for her editorial work and sharing her ideas along the way. Special thanks to Rita Howard, OCD, for special reference work.

Biographical Sketches

Thérèse of Lisieux
  Mary Frances Thérèse Martin was born at Alençon in France on 2 January 1873. At the age of fifteen she obtained permission to enter the Carmelite Monastery of Lisieux. She surrendered herself to God's merciful love, desiring to sacrifice her life for priests and missionaries and the whole Church. She died on 30 September 1887, at the age of twenty-four, promising to "spend my heaven doing good on earth." She was canonized in 1925.

Nicholas the Frenchman
  Little is known of thirteenth-century Nicholas the Frenchman, second prior general of the Order of the Blessed Virgin Mary of Mount Carmel. Three centuries later, his treatise, *The Fiery Arrow*, would serve to strengthen John of the Cross's convictions in the Elijahian spirit of solitude, silence and of the hidden life in Christ through contemplative prayer.

Teresa of Jesus of the Andes
  Juanita Fernancez Solar, (Teresa of Jesus) of Chili, 1900–1920, became the first Latin American Carmelite to be canonized. In his 1993 homily of canonization, Pope John Paul II called her "an eminently contemplative soul" and proposed her as a model for all the world's youth.

Edith Stein (Sr. Benedicta of the Cross)
  Edith Stein was born 12 October 1891. She was a brilliant philosopher, a Carmelite nun, and a Jew, who lost her life in the Auschwitz death camp on 9 August 1942.

Elizabeth of the Trinity
  Elizabeth of the Trinity (Elizabeth Catez) was born on 10 July 1880 in the district of Farges-en-Septain, France. She entered the Carmelite Monastery of Dijon in 1901 and made her profession in 1903. On 9 November 1906 she died; called to light, to love, and to life at the age of twenty-six.

Brother Lawrence of the Resurrection

Brother Lawrence of the Resurrection (Nicolas Herman) was born around the year 1614 in Lorraine, France. He was a lay brother at the Carmelite Monastery on rue de Vaugirard in Paris. He was a humble man who was gifted with the awareness and benefit of the practice of the presence of God. He died in 1691 at the age of seventy-seven.

Teresa of Avila

Teresa of Avila (Teresa de Ahumada y Cepeda) was born on 28 March 1515 at or near Avila, Spain. She entered the Carmelite Monastery of the Incarnation in Avila in 1535. She began preparations for the reform of the order in 1560 after many years of struggle and great graces. From 1562 to 1582 she established numerous foundations across Spain. Teresa died at Alba de Tormes in 1582, was canonized in 1622 and declared a Doctor of the Church in 1970.

John of the Cross

John of the Cross (Juan de Yepes y Alvarez) was born in 1542 at Fontiveros, Spain. He entered the Carmelite Order in 1563. At the request of Teresa of Avila, he joined her in the strict reform of the Carmelite life. He died 13 December 1591. His profound writings on ascetical and mystical theology won him the title of Doctor of the Church.

A Pregnant Silence

*All our sisters, the creatures, which charm our eyes
or ears in solitude, rest us and comfort us. In silence
they sing their beauty and incite us to praise the
admirable Creator.* — *Nicholas the Frenchman**

Stillness is not the absence of motion and silence is not the absence of noise. Stillness and silence are pregnant entities. There is something promising and generative in their presence – something waiting to be birthed. You can feel the heartbeat and the blood flow even though the baby is not yet born.

You recognize stillness when it is there. There is an order to it – things seem to be in right relationship with each other. There can be busyness that is peaceful and noise that is in harmony. In the early morning it is easily perceived as nature begins its day, but the presence of people does not disturb it when love is present. I think it must be the absence of love which disturbs the silence and stillness – upsetting the harmony that seems inherent in the natural universe.

---

* Source: Nicholas the Frenchman, *The Fiery Arrow*, in *Ancient Carmelite Texts*, translations from the Calced Carmelite Fathers used with permission. (Published by Roots Committee, Carmelite Communities Associated, 1982), chap. XI, p. 71.

In Forms Not Always Recognized

After I have known it
love works so in me
that whether things go well or badly
love turns them to one sweetness
transforming the soul in itself. — *John of the Cross**

Our dog, Chewie, died this year. We were buddies. I took care of him and he companioned me. I miss him very much, and I miss the "me" I was when I was with him – the playful, childlike "me" that he called forth.

When we love a person, a pet, a plant, a home, a mountain – whatever it is that transforms us into a more loving self – part of us is given, imperceptibly perhaps, to that other. When that other dies, or the home must be sold, or the mountain left behind, we realize that part of us is missing. The emptiness we feel was the self given, and the self within that only they could evoke.

We have another dog. Her name is Jessica Fletcher – our crime-stopper. I try to spend some time with her each day. Jessie likes to play ball with me. I like to play "fetch"; she prefers "keep away." Sometimes when I am with her I feel playful and childlike again. Transformation and resurrection come subtly and in forms not always recognized. I am content to wait and to believe that someday the self that Chewie called forth will be reborn in me just as I believe that he continues to delight all those who enjoy eternal life.

---

* Source: John of the Cross, *The Poetry*, in *The Collected Works of St. John of the Cross*, trans. Kieran Kavanaugh, OCD, and Otilio Rodriguez, OCD rev. ed. (Washington, DC: ICS Publications, 1991) #11, 3, p. 70.

A Life Surrendered

One must not think that a person who is suffering is
not praying. [S]he is offering up [her] sufferings to
God, and many a time [s]he is praying much more
truly than one who goes away by [her]self and
meditates [her] head off, and, if [s]he has squeezed
out a few tears, thinks that that is prayer.

— *Teresa of Avila*[*]

My mother was a great cook. She loved to entertain family
and friends. She was happiest when she was giving, and she
gave of her time freely. Friends and acquaintances poured out
their troubles to her. She was a good listener. As she grew
older, her delight was to crochet – making scarves and afghans.
She crocheted more than a hundred afghans and gave them all
away. Imperceptibly over time, a kind of numbness began to
affect her extremities – extreme polyneuropathy, the doctor
called it. She lost the use of her hands and feet and she was
confined to the easy chair she once used to relax in. It was her
"home" by day and her bed by night. No longer could her
hands hold pots or pans or her fingers ply the crocheting hook.

The loss of sensation was not the first loss. She had lost a
child, a mother, a husband. Death claimed most of the friends
and neighbors she had enjoyed with phone visits. She would
say in one breath, "I cannot pray anymore," – meaning she
could not pray as she once did – and in another, "Pray? That's
all I can do." I think my mother achieved the prayer of union –
God was her only reality. She never sat in a monastic cell to
make her hours of prayer, or meditated by a river. What she
did was to accept the joys and sorrows of her life and
surrendered to them both – as gifts from God. She lived the
paschal mystery with its daily dyings and risings, and in the
end, she no longer prayed. She *was* prayer.

---

[*] Source: Teresa of Avila, *The Letters of Saint Teresa of Jesus* Vol. I, trans. E.
Allison Peers, (Westminster, Maryland: The Newman Press, 1950), Letter #122,
to Father Jerome Gracian, pp. 316–17.

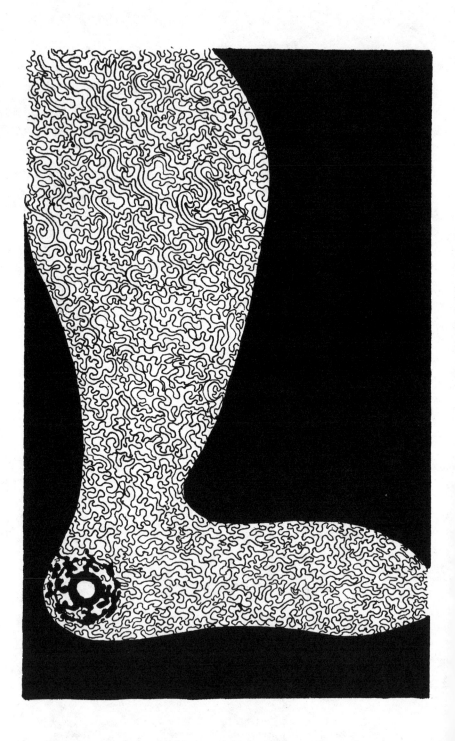

Finding Our God-spot

Consider the human weakness that is consoled by
receiving help in time of need. — *Teresa of Avila**

Of the several versions detailing how Achilles became "invulnerable," the one I like is that in which his mother, the sea-nymph Thetis, held him by the heel dipping him into the river Styx. Wherever the water touched him, Achilles became invulnerable – everywhere but where Thetis had hold of him. I relate to this story. It seems to me it's "our" story – the story of the human condition.

We come into the world very vulnerable, but as we grow older and develop our defenses, we learn how to protect ourselves from others and become somewhat invulnerable. But in God's goodness, we are each given a "God-spot," a place where we are particularly weak, a place of vulnerability. I call it my "original sin," but it is also the place where God has access to my heart. When I feel "all-together" or "on top of things," some incident comes along and hits me in my "God-spot" forcing me to acknowledge my weakness. It keeps me in touch with the human condition, my dependence on God, and those with whom I live. I need this weakness, this Achilles heel. It's the place where God holds me, has access to my heart, connecting me to the One who loved me enough to make me vulnerable.

---

* Source: Teresa of Avila, *The Way of Perfection*, in *The Collected Works of St. Teresa of Avila* Vol. II, trans. Kieran Kavanaugh, OCD, and Otilio Rodriguez, OCD (Washington, DC: ICS Publications, 1980), chap. 1, 6, p. 43.

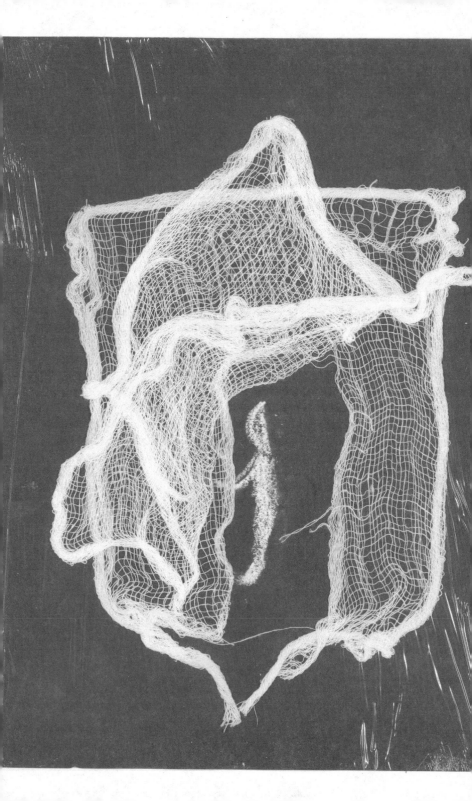

Rising Again

*See that you are not suddenly saddened by the
adversities of this world, for you do not know the good
they bring, being ordained in the judgments of God for
the everlasting joy of the elect.*   — *John of the Cross**

In the creed we say of Jesus, "he was crucified, died and was buried. He descended into hell and on the third day. . . ." I suppose we have all descended into hell at one time or another. My experience of hell has been of rejection and alienation – not necessarily isolation, but times when I felt totally "out of it." I've been there more than once, but God has always searched me out and brought me back on some "third day."

Because of those experiences, I know God will never let go of me. When I descend into hell, God goes with me. Just as I can never be without the Source of my Being, so God cannot be without me – whether I "go up to the heavens or down to the nether world," as the Psalmist says. God's Spirit in the Trinity calls to God's Spirit in me and brings me back. God, who seeks unity and oneness, can never be separated from anything that is.

I pray for my inner self to grow strong, so that I may have the freedom to respond to the creative force within me and not choose the death patterns that are primal within me. I pray to be one with the One, where there can be no alienation. I am grateful for God's constancy and faithfulness, this God who holds me, descends into hell with me, and raises me up as I live out the paschal mystery of life, death, and resurrection.

---

* Source: John of the Cross, *The Sayings of Light and Love,* in *The Collected Works of St. John of the Cross,* trans. Kieran Kavanaugh, OCD, and Otilio Rodriguez, OCD, rev. ed. (Washington, DC: ICS Publications, 1991), 64, p. 90.

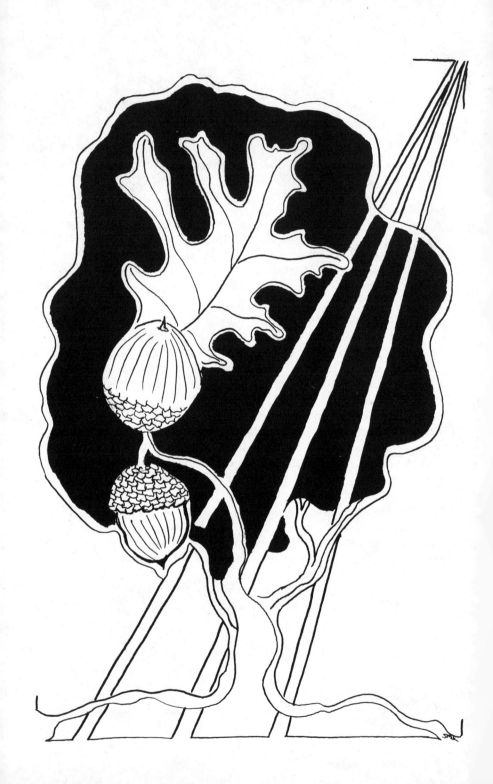

Pebbles in the Pool of Time

The lesson of the past has instructed me for the
future. — *Nicholas the Frenchman*[*]

Time is a strange phenomenon.

There are times we are so absorbed that hours fly by like minutes, and other times we are so bored that minutes seem like hours. Chronological time is deceptive. It gives us the impression that an event is over and done with if it happened sometime in the past. My experience of time has taught me that the past can be a present phenomenon. It is in the present when it is called to memory, and that means that the past can grow and expand. Past hurts can be healed, and slights and rejections can be forgiven even if the one who hurt us is no longer with us.

When I was a child, the atomic bomb was dropped on Hiroshima and I rejoiced! I thought the Japanese were our enemies, the war was over, and we had "won." As I remember the event today, I do not rejoice. The Japanese are not our enemies, and I do not understand what it means "to win a war." That event is not over for me nor for our world. Deformed bodies still live in Hiroshima, and nuclear power is still a concept we wrestle with. Past events are pebbles in the pool of time that continues to ripple out in ever-widening circles as long as memory exists.

On a personal level, that means that the events of my past are not intractable. To the extent that an event of my painful past has not grown or changed, I have not grown or changed. If I still "feel" hurt or resentment, I have not grown or allowed the event to transform me. On the other hand, feelings that are remembered rather than "felt" indicate that the past has grown in me and that I have changed. This is a moment of grace. It means relationships can be healed even if the loved one is dead or out of contact. There is no need to live with regrets for love not given or forgiveness withheld. Every experience, every happening has the potential for being redeemed and transformed, and it is the way each of us can participate in God's power to make all things new.

---

* Source: Nicholas the Frenchman, *The Fiery Arrow*, in *Ancient Carmelite Texts*, translations from the Calced Carmelite Fathers used with permission. (Published by Roots Committee, Carmelite Communities Associated, 1982), chap. XIV, p. 74.

Midnight Moments

*. . . it seems to me that [Jesus] is asking me to live
like [God] 'in an eternal present,' 'with no before, no
after,' but wholly in the unity of my being in this
'eternal now.'* — Elizabeth of the Trinity[*]

Little Bridget was at Mass this morning. She is sixteen
months old and a delight to watch. She lives totally in the
"now." As I watch her, that is where I am also.

When I read of violent crimes, or see a homeless woman
wandering the streets with her grocery cart, or hear a
disoriented man mumbling near a bus stop, I try to picture
them when they were running happily on some school yard, or
learning to ride a bicycle, or toddling around like Bridget. I try
to bring to mind the many children I once taught before I
entered the monastery. Where are they now? Are they among
the homeless or in some jail or are they holding little Bridgets
on their own laps?

When Jesus was born, I don't think Mary or Joseph
thought about anything but the joy of having and holding the
child. At that blessed midnight moment, the future did not
exist: the rejection, betrayal, misunderstanding, the violence of
scourging and crucifixion. There was only joy and gratitude.
What was to come could not impinge on what was present. We
all need times like that – midnight moments – when the
wonder of the present fills our being and the past and the
future cease to exist.

---

[*] Source: Elizabeth of the Trinity, *I Have Found God*, in *Complete Works of
Elizabeth of the Trinity* Vol I, trans. Aletheia Kane, OCD (Washington, DC: ICS
Publications, 1984), #III Last Retreat, 25, p. 152.

Carrying the Christ

O consuming Fire, Spirit of Love, 'come upon me,'
and create in my soul a kind of incarnation of the
Word: that I may be another humanity . . . in which
[this Holy Spirit] can renew [the] whole Mystery.
                              — Elizabeth of the Trinity[*]

Christmas is fast approaching. I love this feast. It is both challenging and comforting. As I read the Scriptures, I hear the message of the annunciation announced to me. The Holy Spirit will come upon me, and the power of the Most High will overshadow me. I who have been barren will be filled with life-giving waters. My kinswomen, too, my community – those I may have perceived as barren – also have been filled and are pregnant with the holy. We are all Christ-bearers. We carry the infant Christ and we carry the suffering Christ as well. At times, Christ is silent in me, moving the Spirit to leap in others, and sometimes the Christ leaps in me as I encounter the Spirit in another.

As a community or as a family, the whole Christ becomes incarnate. In some, Christ comes to birth; in others, Christ advances in age and grace and wisdom. Still others are Christ suffering, or lying in a tomb. To embrace it all is to embrace the whole Christ. Christmas enables me to believe that when Christ is in the tomb of my heart, it is an advent time. The living waters will come and the tomb becomes a womb, waiting to burst forth into a living Christ. Truly, Christmas is our story.

---

* Source: Elizabeth of the Trinity, *I Have Found God*, in *The Complete Works of Elizabeth of the Trinity* Vol. I, trans. Aletheia Kane, OCD (Washington, DC: ICS Publications, 1984), *Prayer*: "O My God, Trinity Whom I Adore," p. 183.

This Unknown Friend

We cannot know whether or not we love God,
although there are strong indications for recognizing
that we do love [God]; but we can know whether we
love our neighbor. — *Teresa of Avila**

I like to pray in the early morning when all is quiet. In the summer, I frequently go outside and walk on the monastery grounds or sit in our courtyard; but in the winter, when the mornings are dark, I prefer to sit in my room, which is very small. The windows are high, so that only the sky and the tops of trees can be seen. Periodically, the blackness is punctuated by the twinkling red and white lights of a passing plane.

I try to picture the travelers going to unknown destinations, and I wrap them in prayer. Where did they begin their journeys? What loved ones wished them well? Who will they meet when they deplane? What calls them to be traveling at this hour? I hold them all in my heart and pray for their safety and their happiness, though they do not know this unknown friend sitting in a monastic cell. Sometimes I wonder if someone looking down on the miniature trees and houses, seeing the lights of the city, is sending down silent blessings upon it – an unknown friend cradling me in prayer. We could be sending arcs of blessing like rainbows, through the skies.

This past year, sixty-eight persons were killed in one plane crash here in Indiana. It was a devastating event. Now as I hear the sound of the engine or see the lights fly past my window, the prayer that rises to enfold them takes on a new importance.

---

* Source: Teresa of Avila, *The Interior Castle*, in *The Collected Works of St. Teresa of Avila* Vol. II, trans. Kieran Kavanaugh, OCD, and Otilio Rodriguez, OCD (Washington, DC: ICS Publications, 1980), V, chap. 3, 8, p. 351.

Coming of Age

*. . . I would counsel those who practice prayer to seek,
at least in the beginning, friendship and association
with other persons having the same interest.*

— *Teresa of Avila**

A year ago I had the privilege of journeying with Dana, a
lovely fifteen-year-old young woman, as she prepared for her
Confirmation. She began the journey as a child with the faith of
her parents and ended it a woman, with conviction – an adult
Christian. I think that might also be the story of the boy Jesus,
who at twelve went up to Jerusalem and was so captivated by
his encounter in the temple that he became lost in God,
returning to Nazareth a young man. That is what Confirmation
or Bar/Bat Mitzvah or other religious initiation ceremonies are
to symbolize – the passage from the acceptance of a child to the
faith of an adult.

This is not a one-time happening. As I continue my own
journey, I continue in self-revelation. God continues to reveal
me to myself, so that I can know both my "girl-child" and my
"woman-child." God reveals to me and enables me to
appreciate that I am indeed, child of God, a creature and a
sinner, finite and imperfect. This revelation enables my
"girl-child" to crawl up into God's lap and to be held and
loved, knowing that at times I am called to leave behind the
ways of the "girl-child" in the temple of God's embrace. It
empowers me to let the "woman-child" emerge with
self-knowledge, holding the child with compassion and
forgiveness. It is a reminder that we are never too old to come
of age and to grow in wisdom and grace.

---

* Source: Teresa of Avila, *The Book of Her Life*, in *The Collected Works of St.
Teresa of Avila* Vol. I, trans. Kieran Kavanaugh, OCD, and Otilio Rodriguez,
OCD rev. ed (Washington, DC: ICS Publications, 1987), chap. 7, 20, p. 92.

Demon or Angel?

*Let us look at our own faults and leave aside those of
others. . . . Perhaps we could truly learn from the one
who shocks us what is most important.*

— Teresa of Avila[*]

After his baptism, Matthew tells us that Jesus was led by
the Spirit into the desert in order to be tempted. I've often
wondered about that. We had just been told he was the
"beloved Son in whom God was well pleased." Why did he
need to be tempted? Was it to learn his own powerlessness, his
weakness, his total dependence on God? He was a young man
of thirty years, full of zeal. Did he need to face his own
helplessness, his own creatureliness, his own vulnerability?

I like to think of him there roaming about for forty days
with little or nothing to eat or drink. As time wore on, I
imagine he looked a bit wild, his hair dirty, his clothes tattered.
Did he look like the outcasts, the lepers, the unclean, the
tormented women and men who roamed the desert with him;
those who were not allowed to be with the acceptable people of
his society? Did he see their tortured eyes, their hopelessness,
possibly their ministry to one another? And when he had
reached his limit of endurance, could not the angels who
ministered to him have been those very outcasts, or perhaps
some Samaritans passing along the way – those unacceptable
"others." Maybe it was this experience that gave Jesus a new
vision, a new mission: to give sight to the blind, to heal the
sick, to free the oppressed.

When I experience my own desert-times – times of
alienation, barrenness, or aloneness, I tend to forget that I may
have been led there by the Spirit to face my own demons, to let
them emerge and rise before me, and to learn my own
powerlessness and weakness, to enable me to see my oneness
with others who feel alienated, rejected, barren, alone. I need to

---

[*] Source: Teresa of Avila, *The Interior Castle*, in *The Collected Works of St. Teresa
of Avila* Vol. II, trans. Kieran Kavanaugh, OCD and Otilio Rodriguez, OCD
(Washington, DC: ICS Publications, 1980) III, chap. 2, 13, p. 315.

recognize and acknowledge those whom I have "kept at a distance" as those who can broaden my vision, who can stretch my boundaries and free me from the trap of judging who or what is "acceptable." My demons can minister to me if I acknowledge them, and those others whom I hold at a distance may well be the angels who will bring me to wholeness.

In Return Nothing Gains All

She employs all her faculties and possessions in
loving, in giving up everything like the wise merchant
[Mt. 13:44], for this treasure of love has been found by
her, hidden in God.   — *John of the Cross**

One of my favorite outings is a trip to the zoo. There is so much to learn from watching the different animals. There are signs that alert the viewer to specific behaviors to watch at particular exhibits. As you visit the baboons, a sign reads: "You scratch my back and I'll scratch yours." Baboons do a lot of that!

But reciprocity is not something we as humans can anticipate. Sometimes we have a hidden expectation, such as: I sent them a Christmas card, so they should send me one; or, I asked them to dinner, so they should invite me! But reciprocity is not a Christian virtue. According to the gospel, we are called to love our enemies and to do good to those who persecute us. To be a Christian, therefore, means at times accepting the challenge of detaching ourselves from our fondest desires!

Among our fondest desires are those of being accepted, understood, loved, living in a life-giving environment, and having our talents recognized and used. These desires are not wrong, but if we are not detached from them, we will never find peace of heart.

To be loved, accepted, appreciated, treated justly depends on the "other" over whom I have no control! What *happens* to me is far different from what I *make happen*. Love, justice, acceptance are not of themselves reciprocal. We may scratch someone's back, but that does not mean she or he will scratch ours! God is an unconditional lover and a prodigal forgiver. God does not wait on our "worthiness" to lavish love and forgiveness upon us, and we who are made in God's image are called to a non-reciprocal love, a non-reciprocal forgiveness, a non-reciprocal acceptance. To be followers of Christ is to choose to embrace a crucified life with a resurrected heart.

---

* Source: John of the Cross, *The Spiritual Canticle*, in *The Collected Works of St. John of the Cross*, trans. Kieran Kavanaugh, OCD, and Otilio Rodriguez, OCD rev. ed. (Washington, DC: ICS Publications, 1991), Stanza 27, 8, p. 583.

Prayer Is a Door

. . . the door of entry to this castle is prayer and reflection. — *Teresa of Avila*[*]

We live in a time filled with renewed interest in prayer by persons of all faiths. At the same time, ours is an age in which we are bombarded with so many material desires which distract us in our search for God.

Prayer enables us to live a more focused life. We experience transformation as we grow in the experience of God's love. Selfishness gives way to selflessness; pride is exposed; and the desire for a simpler, more humble life increases. Little by little God draws us and we respond. The call to prayer, solitude and spiritual reading becomes stronger. Concern for the poor and the underprivileged deepens. Increasingly, God becomes the focus of our relationships.

The journey is challenging at times, and we may be tempted to turn back. But if we continue to respond to God's gentle call, we grow in faith and in love. God will become a personal God who is always present to us. Peace and trust will persist even in darkness. God will truly be rooted at the center of our being, a Person whom we meet face to face, heart to heart.

---

[*] Source: Teresa of Avila, *The Interior Castle,* in *The Collected Works of St. Teresa of Avila*, Vol. II, trans. Kieran Kavanaugh, OCD and Otilio Rodriguez, OCD. (Washington, DC: ICS Publications, 1980) I, chap. 1, 7, p. 286.

The Gift of Everything

God asks our all, and we must give What [God] did
first bestow. . . .   — *Thérèse of Lisieux*[*]

My niece, Maureen, was a beautiful young woman of twenty-nine. She had so much going for her: a happy marriage, a precious little baby boy and a computer position at UPS that challenged her in every way. She loved life, her family, her friends and her work. In the eyes of the world she was a successful young woman with everything to live for.

In early December, 1993, she was diagnosed with osteo-sarcoma of the jaw, a rare type of cancer. It was hard to believe this beautiful young woman who looked the picture of health could really be so sick. The news was a shock to her and her family, but she worked toward acceptance from the outset. Her concerns were for others: her husband, baby, family, friends and co-workers, the nurses, and those who cared for her. She had radiation to her jaw prior to the scheduled radical surgery. Then the real bombshell came – brain cancer! The doctors were unable to get it all. Surgery and radiation did help for a period of time, but after some months, the doctors told her that nothing more could be done. She returned home to the loving care of Hospice and her devoted family.

Life can be changed in an instant. But as with tragedies, deaths and losses of every kind in our lives, we have choices. Maureen, who is a faith-filled woman, chose to turn to God and to those who loved her for her strength to live each day to the fullest, knowing that God is in charge. She understood that her responsibility was to work toward acceptance and to be a hopeful presence to others. At times, the going was rough, but like Job she trusted in God. She said to me: "God is always there for me. The short time I've had, has been filled with happiness – a loving husband, the joy of motherhood, wonderful friends and co-workers who have followed me through this journey to new life." And in a letter to the community she wrote: "Jesus is truly my Savior, and with God's help I can certainly get through this. I have given God all

---

* Source: *Experiencing St. Thérèse Today*, in *Carmelite Studies* Vol. 5, edited by John Sullivan, OCD, (Washington, DC: ICS Publications, 1990), quotation from article, *Thérèse and the Modern Temperament* by Barry Ulanov, p. 160.

my fears, anxieties and pains, and although I still worry at times, I can feel the strength of God pulling me through."

It is the middle of Lent, both figuratively and in reality, as I write the reflection and I await the word of Maureen's resurrection to new life. The thought of her impending death is very painful, but I rejoice at the legacy she will leave. I feel I will have a niece and friend in heaven who is very present through the communion of saints.

Maureen's example sheds light on what holiness really is in this life. She has opened herself to God and has graciously permitted God to take away whatever God desires. Her total gift of acceptance, love and concern for others is an eternal flame in the minds and hearts of those who love her.

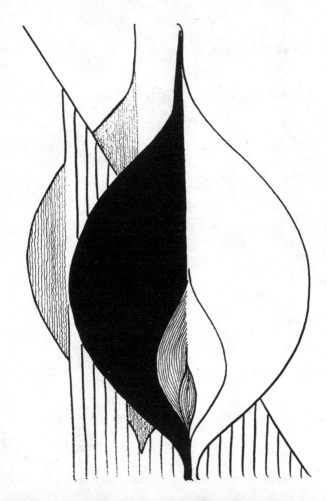

God Hears My Heart

Let us speak to the heart words bathed in sweetness
and love that do indeed please you [God]. . . .
— *John of the Cross*[*]

My God hears my heart
Its formless tears
Its silent longings
Its scarred memories.

My God hears and heals my heart
and
sends out feelings of love and gratitude
and
touchings of compassion.

My God hears my heart
and teaches it to laugh.

---

[*] Source: John of the Cross, *The Sayings of Light and Love,* in *The Collected Works of St. John of the Cross,* trans. Kieran Kavanaugh, OCD, and Otilio Rodriguez, OCD, rev. ed. (Washington, DC: ICS Publications, 1991), Prologue, p. 85.

God of Re-cycling

*The soul's center is God. When it has reached God
with all the capacity of its being and the strength of
its operation and inclination, it will have attained its
final and deepest center in God, it will know, love and
enjoy God with all its might.* — John of the Cross[*]

Crushed cereal boxes,
Rejected paper,
Plastic packaging and wrapping.
Each piece needs to be examined, categorized,
    before taken to the local re-cycling center,
center of rejuvenation,
junction of hope for our over-burdened planet

God most willingly accepts
    each crushed dream,
    each rejected hope,
    all of our "plastic," superfluous selfish wants and needs.
If we are willing to examine and change
    God recycles our motives – our moments
    with forgiveness.
We again are lovingly rejuvenated.

---

[*] Source: John of the Cross, *The Living Flame of Love*, in *The Collected Works of
St. John of the Cross*, trans. Kieran Kavanaugh, OCD, and Otilio Rodriguez,
OCD rev. ed. (Washington, DC: ICS Publications, 1991), Commentary on
Stanza 1, 12, p. 645.

Searching for Signs

Those who now desire to question God or receive some
vision or revelation are guilty not only of foolish
behavior but also of offending [God]. . . .
— *John of the Cross**

I recall a homilist telling the story of a believer who attempted to discern God's will through the practice of "Bible Roulette." Prayerfully she took her Bible and arbitrarily opened to what she hoped would be words of direction. Her first attempt landed her at Matthew 27:5, speaking of Judas' actions after the betrayal: "He went off and hanged himself." Convinced of the need for a second attempt, she closed her Bible and then opened it up again, this time to Jesus' words: "Go and do likewise." Needless to say, she decided to put her Bible away and to explore God's will through other means.

Humorous as this story may be, I think many of us find ourselves searching for supernatural signs to point the way. I remember one of my own feeble attempts about a year ago. It was January 16 and I was in Los Angeles, trying to decide whether to accept a job offer there. I had no desire to live in Los Angeles, but I *was* in need of a job and I had to make a decision right away. After church that morning, I decided to ask the priest to pray over me for enlightenment and direction. I remember his words clearly, "Please, dear God, send some sign of your will for her life."

I went to bed that night, still undecided about what to do. Six hours into my sleep, I awoke to the sound of dogs barking, car alarms ringing and the room shaking. The Los Angeles earthquake was upon me! As I was fumbling for my glasses and bathrobe, I remember one of the many thoughts that went through my mind: "Boy, is that priest a powerful pray-er! This is sign enough for me; I'm out of here!"

---

* Source: John of the Cross, *The Ascent of Mount Carmel,*in *The Collected Works of St. John of the Cross*, trans. Kieran Kavanaugh, OCD, and Otilio Rodriguez, OCD rev. ed. (Washington, DC: ICS Publications, 1991) Book Two, chap. 22, 5, p. 230.

Was it foolish of me to have asked for direction? No, I don't believe so. Jesus assured us that if we knock, the door will be opened to us. The foolishness, it seems, is in constantly scanning the horizon for supernatural signs. God, it turns out, speaks to us in much more direct, concrete ways. In my case, I ended up staying in Los Angeles. The freeway I needed to take to my alternate destination had collapsed and there was no other route available to me. Humorous, indeed, are God's ways!

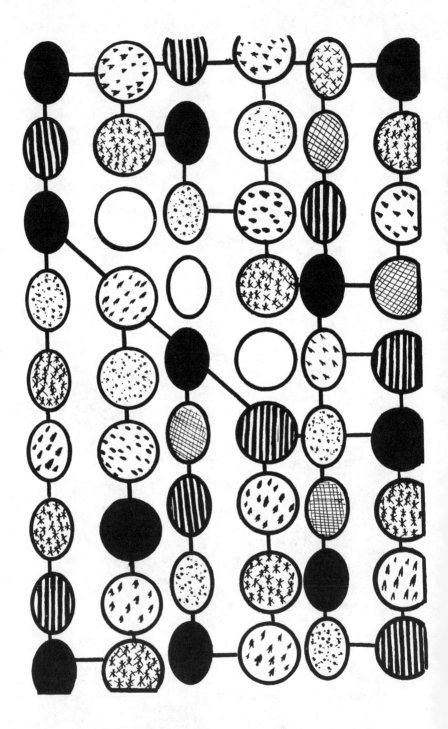

Empty Spaces

If I had had a little faith, I wouldn't have experienced
any disturbance. . . . — *Teresa of Avila**

On those not so infrequent occasions when I find myself lacking in faith, I think back to an episode last year when I was in the car with my sister and five-year-old nephew. We were in a parking lot, trying to find an empty space. When my sister spotted one close to the store entrance, she exclaimed, "Hey look! There's a space. I guess there's a God after all!" Without hesitation, my nephew spoke up and said, "Of course there's a God, Mommy."

If only we adults could hold onto the innocent faith of youth. Perhaps that faith is first shattered when we are told the awful truth about Santa Claus. All of a sudden the world doesn't seem quite as secure and assured as we once thought. Fortunately or unfortunately, that seems to be a lesson we learn over and over again as we proceed through life.

It's not the existence of God that I find problematic; life has provided me with sufficient evidence of it. The issue for me is how closely God is involved in my day-to-day life. Whether it's parking spaces or healing a friend's illness, it's an ongoing debate between happenstance or divine intention. For me, it doesn't seem to be a debate that will be easily resolved. Rather, it is a mystery that will be carried with me throughout life. As I struggle with the mystery, though, I will try to remember the certainty of my nephew's response. Perhaps it will serve to strengthen me in my journey of faith.

---

* Source: Teresa of Avila, *The Book of Her Life,* in *The Collected Works of St. Teresa of Avila* Vol. I, trans. Kieran Kavanaugh, OCD, and Otilio Rodriguez, OCD rev. ed (Washington, DC: ICS Publications, 1987), chap. 36, 16, p. 316.

Pride – The Dividing Line

*I have understood that what most keeps me from God
is my pride. From now on I desire and propose to be
humble.* — *Teresa of the Andes*[*]

True humility is an ambitious goal for most of us; pride
comes much more easily. As I look back on my life, I can see
how pride has kept me not only from God but from a full life
as well.

Pride is a dividing line, hindering us in our relationships.
The most perilous dividing line, of course, is the one that
separates us from God. I lived in that separation for several
years. All it took was a mild dose of existentialist reading
toward the end of high school. Then at the advanced age of
seventeen, I concluded that God was beneath me, a crutch
needed only by the unenlightened masses.

Time has taught me otherwise. God, it turned out, was not
a crutch but a gift and a challenge to the mediocrity of life. The
question I have pondered is how to convey this realization to
those who continue on the other side of the divide. Perhaps I
can't; the matter is in God's hands.

God's call is ever-present, manifest in many ways.
However, it often takes humility to recognize and respond to
that call. The answer for me, therefore, is in praying that like
myself, others may let go of their pride and allow God to
bridge love's divide.

---

* Source: Teresa of the Andes, *GOD, THE JOY OF MY LIFE*, trans. Michael D.
Griffin, OCD, (Washington, DC: ICS Publications, 1989), Diary 1900–1914, #29
(retreat of 1917), p. 156.

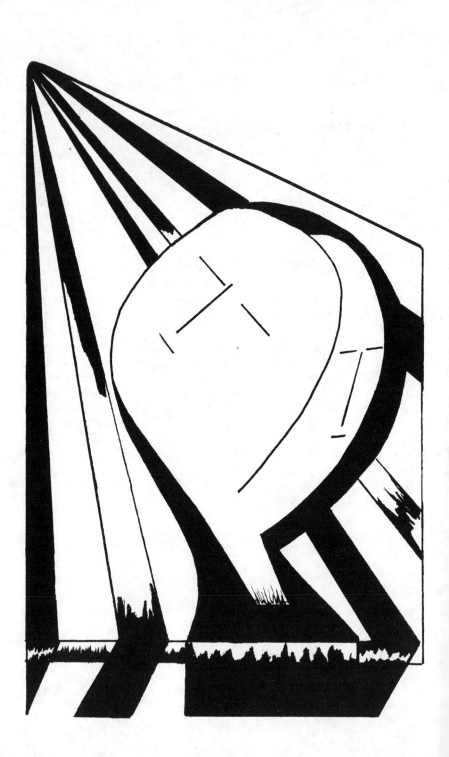

May We Know Ourselves

Test us, Lord – for You know the truth – so that we
may know ourselves.   *— Teresa of Avila** *

Self-knowledge was a key component of Teresa's formula for spiritual development. Indeed, to her growth in knowledge of self and growth in knowledge of God were considered equally important. Since overlooked strengths and weaknesses impair Christian service, Teresa saw self-knowledge as a means to an end, not an end in itself.

Teresa saw self-knowledge as an integral part of God's plan for the world's redemption. God alone knows truth, both on a cosmic and personal level, and it is only through the unfolding of global and individual histories that this truth is made known.

As salvation history makes clear, it is God's testing which makes this unfold. Abraham and Sarah leave their homeland, and humanity advances in faith. Job surrenders to the mystery of tribulation, and humanity advances in humility. Jesus forgives his executioners, and humanity advances in compassion.

We see these advances in our individual lives as well. We seek wholeness, but are only partially aware of what impedes our inner unity. However, God tests us so that our vision might be made clear. Often such tests parallel the tests of history. Like Abraham and Sarah, we may be asked to leave the familiar behind in response to God's call. Like Job, we may be asked to accept apparently meaningless suffering. Like Jesus, we may be challenged to return love for rejection. Painful though they may be, such tests clarify just how shallow or deep our virtues run.

God therefore allows self-knowledge to evolve naturally as our own truths are gradually made known. We experience the tests and, whatever the outcome, we pray for increased wisdom. We pray, too, for the grace to recognize the tests, the grace to embrace and grow from the testing, and most importantly, the grace to put its outcome to the service of love.

---

* Source: Teresa of Avila, *The Interior Castle*, in *The Collected Works of St. Teresa of Avila* Vol. II, trans. Kieran Kavanaugh, OCD, and Otilio Rodriguez, OCD (Washington, DC: ICS Publications, 1980), III, chap. 1, 9, p. 309.

Chosen People

Those who are in the city, being chosen people, are
such that they can do more by themselves than many
cowardly soldiers can. — *Teresa of Avila**

We learn something about ourselves through what is asked of us. Whether it is the thrill of a request to sharpen the teacher's pencils at the age of six or the responsibility of being elected CEO at sixty, there is a message here. We can grow or wither on the summons of life, on the way that we are recognized by others.

Every person bears the responsibility of stewardship for life itself. People of every faith are inspired to witness to the reality of God in their lives; Christians are urged to live the message of the gospel. But these serious, foundational invitations can become so familiar that we can forget that they are a call – to us.

Recently I realized that for years I have been praying with and for people who are involved in international organizations. They had asked for my support, and I have been happy to respond. Only now do I realize the call this has been for me. God and they had recognized me. How had I responded?

Far from being an occasion of self-satisfaction, the question challenged me to ask myself how I have measured up. That sent shock waves through the remembrance of all of my calls, the life-long generic ones and the short-term requests that come to me during each day. It was an opportunity to realize that everything we are asked to do counts. We are all "chosen people." We need only listen for the call.

---

* Source: Teresa of Avila, *The Way of Perfection*, in *The Collected Works of St. Teresa of Avila* Vol. II, trans. Kieran Kavanaugh, OCD, and Otilio Rodriguez, OCD (Washington, DC: ICS Publications, 1980), chap. 3, 1, p. 48.

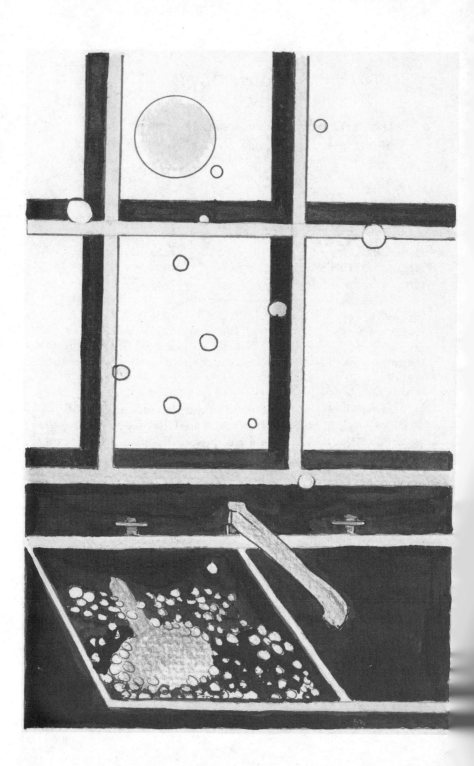

One Timeless Gift

. . . the Lord walks among the pots and pans. . . .
— *Teresa of Avila*[*]

In this single sentence, Teresa alerts us to the mystery of the abiding presence of the Holy Spirit within each of us. This is the Spirit that prays in us when we do not know what to ask for. It is the mystery that enables us to pray always and everywhere.

Our work need not be a distraction from our presence to God. It is the very milieu in which God works through us. After making the intention to remain in the Divine Presence no matter what we are doing, we need only keep God in mind as the task at hand allows.

Pictures on a wall or desk, billboards we see on the way to work, as well as occurrences such as the chiming of a clock, getting caught in a long line at a checkout counter, or interruptions that break our train of thought – all of these can become reminders of the presence of God.

We cannot always be conscious of the Divine Presence, but our hearts can be dedicated to God at work or play as well as at times especially given to prayer. In these latter times of solitary quiet prayer, we can make the conscious acceptance of all that we are in God and say yes to all that life has in store for us. This conscious commitment is the core that unites all that we are and do into one timeless gift of ourselves to God. Then whatever we are doing, we carry the assurance that we are in the Lord.

---

[*] Source: Teresa of Avila, *The Book of Her Foundations*, in *The Collected Works of St. Teresa of Avila* Vol. III, trans. Kieran Kavanaugh, OCD, and Otilio Rodriguez, OCD, (Washington, DC: ICS Publications, 1985), chap. 5, 8, pp. 119–120.

Friends for "Life"

This good company began to help me get rid of the habits that the bad company had caused. . . .

— *Teresa of Avila*[*]

As a growing girl St. Teresa had to deal with a new wave of materialism that stemmed from Spain's success in the Americas. She had time on her hands and a few cousins who liked to live it up. This did not add up to a rich recipe for spiritual growth. Teresa fed her mind with romance novels and joined the crowd until she was finally blessed with a good companion who spoke to her of God and who seriously influenced her life.

I am always a little surprised at my own inner response to reading the lives of the saints or to meeting someone who is living an exemplary life. A new energy is released and I am changed. Something in me seems to say that I can do more with my life too.

It is reminiscent of the days when piano lessons were beginning to drag. A chance concert, even on the radio, would stir my imagination about what I might be able to do with the instrument.

Excellence can magnetize and inspire us; evil and the mediocre also have their lure. Teresa challenges us about where we are placing ourselves and what we are feeding our minds. Who are our heroes and where do we encounter them? Did she ever dream that she would be one of them?

---

[*] Source: Teresa of Avila, *The Book of Her Life*, in *The Collected Works of St. Teresa of Avila* Vol. I, trans. Kieran Kavanaugh, OCD, and Otilio Rodriguez, OCD, rev. ed. (Washington, DC: ICS Publications, 1987), chap. 3, 1, p. 61.

Unfinished Saints

*I pointed [the stars] out to Papa and told him my
name was written in heaven.* — Thérèse of Lisieux*

Unlike most other saints, Thérèse of Lisieux did not dwell on the fact that she was not perfect. St. Teresa of Avila referred to herself as a worm as did the psalmist, but Thérèse called herself a little flower. She considered herself not so much a sinner as an unfinished saint. If we use the example of the glass being half full or half empty, she chose the more positive view. She took the life that God gave her and ran with it.

Biographers of Thérèse make much of the fact that she had more than enough familial love in her childhood, which surely helped her develop a deep faith in a loving God. The fact that Thérèse has found such universal popularity, however, seems to indicate that the faithful do not allow this early advantage to overshadow her heroism. She had her share of suffering throughout her life, and she died a slow and painful death.

Holiness, like life, is a gift. Our part in both is cooperation. I suspect that people are drawn to Thérèse because of what she did with what she had. We may not have been born into supremely loving families but most of us have known some degree of love sometime in our lives. If we recall the gospel parable of the talents, Thérèse's life reminds us that whatever degree of love we have received was meant to be invested and multiplied rather than buried under the unloves that are also in the package of our lives.

Perhaps the attraction is even deeper. Perhaps Thérèse lets us know that whatever our performance, the very longing of our hearts is God's invitation to continue to live and love in hope, if even in a "little way." But then isn't that what Thérèse's story is all about?

---

* Source: Thérèse of Lisieux, *Manuscript A*, in *Story of a Soul/The Autobiography of St. Thérèse of Lisieux*, trans. John Clarke, OCD, (Washington, DC: ICS Publications, 1975), chap. 2, p. 43.

Dying Daily

*And I who desired martyrdom, is it possible that I
should die in bed!*   — *Thérèse of Lisieux**

Though martyrdom is inspiring, few of us aspire to it as
did St. Thérèse. Giving one's life is surely the limit in
expressions of faith, and the world is richer for those who have
so offered themselves. Most of us will never merit the alleluias
that accompany the canonization of a martyr, but I believe that
there is much to be said about the daily manifestations of faith
of the average person.

Consider the congregation at liturgy on a given Sunday.
Here is a woman who comes early and enters by the side door
that offers a ramp for her invalid husband's wheelchair. There
is the father of four whose wife was recently diagnosed with
cancer. The couple in back is mourning the death of their
newborn, and the mother on the aisle is weeping for her son
who was just arrested in a drug raid.

The lives of these sisters and brothers of ours bear living
witness to their faith. As St. Paul writes, they "die daily," but
by remaining faithful to their hope in God, they light our way
as surely as the martyrs have done.

It is well to remember that while we attend the liturgy to
praise God, we are there also to support one another by our
prayers, our presence, and our care. Together we are the Body
of Christ, a suffering body that can rise to the challenges of life
through the ministry of its members.

Although she lived in a cloister and was finally confined
to an early sick-bed, St. Thérèse aspired to be love in the heart
of the church, and she was eventually named the patron of the
missions.

Like St. Thérèse most of us will die in our beds. Like her,
too, we can touch the whole world with our lives through our
prayers, our desires, and our heartfelt care for others.

---

* Source: Thérèse of Lisieux, *The "Yellow Notebook" of Mother Agnes,* in *St.
Thérèse of Lisieux/Her Last Conversations,* trans. John Clarke, OCD, (Washington,
DC: ICS Publications, 1977), August 4, #7, p. 132.

First Confession

It was [my little mother] who received all my intimate confidences and cleared up all my doubts.

— Thérèse of Lisieux[*]

It has been over fifty years since I made my first confession, but I still remember the words of one of my classmates. With utter candor, he told me that his mother had "made his list of sins" for him. I was several years older than Jim and had labored long and seriously over my own list. I was impressed then, and I am even more impressed now. I envision a discussion beginning something like this:

Jim: Mom, our First Communion class has to go to confession tomorrow, and I don't know what to say.

Mom: Jim, do you remember when I asked you yesterday if you had looked in on Grandma on the way home from school? You said that you had, but you hadn't.

Jim: Oh, yes. I did that. I lied, and that was a sin.

I heard then and remember now with envy the trust inherent in Jim's preparation for confession. This is the Eden story completely undone. No room here for Satan's great lie that makes God either a competitor or a damning judge. "What have I done? Yes, I did it," says this new Adam.

Admittedly St. Thérèse remembered her sins with a slightly more delicate conscience than Jim, but his total confidence in his mother's love and acceptance of him – sins and all – surely mirrors Thérèse's view of God which was also gleaned from her family.

Freely admitting our failures to others, to God, and to ourselves may not come naturally to some of us, but the saints and some children are there to show us the way. St. Paul tells us that Jesus is the image of the invisible God. This image, this Jesus hangs with arms outstretched for and to us who fail daily. What more could he have done to merit our trust?

---

[*] Source: Thérèse of Lisieux, *Manuscript A*, in STORY OF A SOUL/*The Autobiography of St. Thérèse of Lisieux*, trans. John Clarke, OCD, (Washington, DC: ICS Publications, 1975), chap. 2, p. 44.

Don't Waste Pain

Remember how many sick people there are who are
poor and have no one to complain to. . . .
— *Teresa of Avila**

A founding member of our community died recently, and after the tributes and all that funerals entail had subsided, I took some time to think about what her death meant to me. I recalled her words about finding the nursing home a growth experience, and that she had been excited about the fact that one is never too old to be stretched.

As I thought about this I was surprised to find myself caught up in the memory of Archbishop Oscar Romero. The movie about him shows him thrown into a barrio one rainy night as he was attempting to mediate between the poor and rich of El Salvador. He wandered through the mud and rain as shabbily clad women and children watched him from the doors of their pitiful shacks. That night, he too, was stretched.

I began to realize the possibilities for conversion that might lie in every new or painful situation. Another of Sister's sayings came back to me. "Don't waste pain. Make it work for you." One way that we might make it do this for us is to observe what is happening to us in the process, to listen for signs of new invitations to growth or new life.

Teresa of Avila had a feel for this, too. When her sisters complained of the hardships of cloistered life, she was quick to compare their hardships with those suffered by their sisters "in the world." Not only the once-in-a-lifetime experiences call us to conversion. Daily life is full of such calls. The smallest inconvenience that throws our routine off balance is enough to open our eyes to something new if we are willing to see it. "What, no coffee?" or "The battery is dead?"

"Don't waste pain. Make it work for you."

* Source: Teresa of Avila, *The Way of Perfection*, in *The Collected Works of St. Teresa of Avila* Vol. II, trans. Kieran Kavanaugh, OCD, and Otilio Rodriguez, OCD (Washington, DC: ICS Publications, 1980), chap. 11, 3, p. 80.

Luring God's Glance

Where have you hidden,
Beloved, and left me moaning?
You fled like the stag
after wounding me;
I went out calling you, but you were gone.

Shepherds, you who go
up through the sheepfolds to the hill,
if by chance you see
him I love most,
tell him I am sick, I suffer, and I die.

— *John of the Cross*[*]

The *Spiritual Canticle* invites us to realize that our life with God is a process. There was a beginning. Once it was this way, but now it is not. What happened? Will there be a future? Once prayer felt great, now I feel nothing. Was there really ever anything or anyone? This is faith language. To believe or not to believe. It is also hope language. Can I hold onto the memory of God's call?

The good news! The wounded one is "moaning." The wounded one has been touched by God, has tasted, in however slight a way, the loving presence of God, and for whatever reason, this is gone now. The absence is experienced as a wound, and the lover in this poem is not an indifferent victim. There is a felt loss here, and the deeper the feeling, the less likely one is to let it go or to deny that there ever was a relationship or an encounter. In fact, the very longing is the Presence of God luring the soul to deeper intimacy.

The better news! The lost one is searching and asking for help. "Shepherds . . . if by chance you see. . . ." In his commentary, John says that the person is not demanding in asking for help. The pray-er knows that this relationship is up

---

[*] Source: John of the Cross, *The Spiritual Canticle*, in *The Collected Works of St. John of the Cross*, trans. Kieran Kavanaugh, OCD, and Otilio Rodriguez, OCD rev. ed. (Washington, DC: ICS Publications, 1991) The Poem, stanzas 1–2, p. 471.

to God's initiative and that she is the receiver from beginning to end. But that does not diminish the persistence of the search.

The best news! The abandoned one is communicating. The one who seems to have lost all contact with the Beloved is hiding nothing. "Tell him that I sicken, suffer, and die." Jesus tells us that he has come for the sick, not for those who are well. John has the soul expose all the pain of the wound in order to lure a healing glance from the Beloved. The desire for union must be kept alive, and in John's mind, everything at hand must be employed to keep that desire at white heat.

One Body

*Everything seems to be a heavy burden, and rightly
so, because it involves a war against ourselves.*

— *Teresa of Avila**

During World War II just about everything one purchased
was either hard to find or rationed. Patriotism was high, and
few complained because we all knew that our sisters and
brothers in the armed services were doing without, and we
wanted to be one with them in the war effort. Scarce items that
were acquired honestly were neither flaunted nor hoarded, and
those who got what they wanted through the "black market"
were considered traitors of sorts. There was a war going on.

Today we speak of a war on poverty, on drugs, or on
crime. In some way the causes of all the underprivileged –
minority races, women, children, the disabled, all who are less
than free to live fully human lives – also call for a declaration
of war against the evils that enslave.

We are all involved in these causes, for we are one in the
same human race, the same Body of Christ. For those of us who
are free, searching out our part and responding properly
contributes to that heavy burden, that "war against ourselves"
that St. Teresa writes about. But searching and warring within
ourselves can be a grace in itself, for Teresa also writes that
once we begin to enter this war effort, God grants us many
favors and our labor seems very light.

"Take my yoke upon you and learn of me, for I am meek
and humble of heart; my yoke is easy and my burden light,"
says Jesus. Heavy burden, war within, or war without – all are
made light in communion with Christ who carried the burdens
of us all.

---

* Source: Teresa of Avila, *The Way of Perfection*, in *The Collected Works of St. Teresa of Avila* Vol. II, trans. Kieran Kavanaugh, OCD, and Otilio Rodriguez, OCD (Washington, DC: ICS Publications, 1980), chap. 12, 1, p. 81.

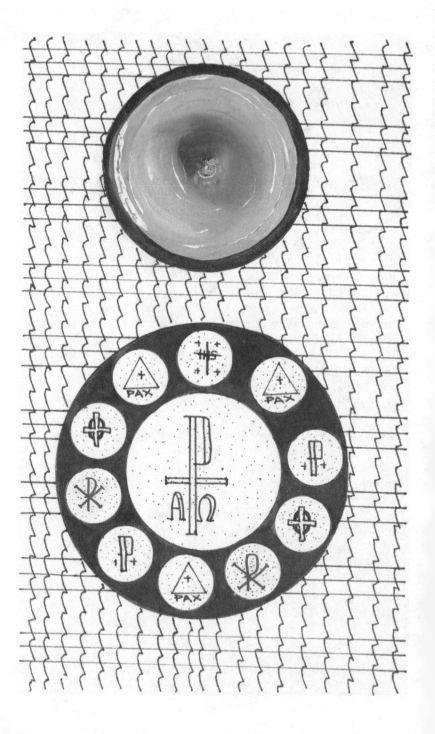

Seeing from Afar

If I were in another Carmel, what difference would it make to me if they cut down entirely all the chestnut trees in the Carmel of Lisieux! — Thérèse of Lisieux[*]

When St. Thérèse found herself struggling with a difference of opinion with her sisters in the monastery, she sometimes imagined herself in another community where she would be able to evaluate the conflict from afar. Seen from a distance the situation was drained of its irritation, and she was able to smile at the importance that she had placed upon it up close.

There is something to be said for this approach. Occasionally we are challenged "to rise above" a difficulty. If I imagine that I am looking down on myself as I experience a situation, I find that while I am at once totally present to all involved, I can simultaneously monitor my actions while I am "on top of" the pull of emotions that could limit my freedom. I can deflate the negative energies from afar and give my best response.

How often we leave an incident and after thinking about it, wish we could do it all over again. Using one's imagination, as St. Thérèse suggests, gives us that second chance at the moment. We are there with the advantage of seeing from afar. We give ourselves time to be our best – one of St. Thérèse's "little ways" of being big about things.

[*] Source: Thérèse of Lisieux, *The "Yellow Notebook" of Mother Agnes,* in *ST. THÉRÈSE OF LISIEUX/Her Last Conversations,* trans. John Clarke, OCD, (Washington, DC: ICS Publications, 1977), September 24, #2, p. 197.

This Graced Cycle

Let yourself be loved . . . .   — Elizabeth of the Trinity

Knees up.
Knees down.
Pedals, chain and wheel in turn, turn.

Knees up.
Knees down.
Pedals, chain and wheel in turn, turn . . . .

As with the pattern of the exercise bike, so in my
relationship with God:
God loves me.
I feel loved.
I love others.

God loves me.
I feel loved.
I love others . . . .

This graced cycle is only broken when
I neglect loving myself,
Forget that others love me,
Forget that God loves me unconditionally – even if my
feet slip.

If my pace quickens or slows,
If I'm up or I'm down,
GOD LOVES ME!
GOD LOVES ME!
GOD LOVES ME!

---

* Source: Elizabeth of the Trinity, *I Have Found God*, in *Complete Works of
Elizabeth of the Trinity* Vol I, trans. Aletheia Kane, OCD (Washington, DC: ICS
Publications, 1984), #IV Let Yourself Be Loved, 2, p. 179.

Humble Me, O God

Humility does not disturb or disquiet or agitate,
however great it may be; it comes with peace, delight,
and calm.   — *Teresa of Avila**

Life continually presents us with opportunities for learning humility. I experienced one such opportunity recently. It was a powerful experience, both freeing and humorous.

I had been in a group discussion and was struggling with the variety of ideological and theological opinions which had been expressed. I was particularly perplexed with those who seemed to want to see God only at their own level. After discussing this with a friend, I decided to take my concerns to prayer.

I knew the problem was with me and not with those whom I was questioning. Why, I wondered in prayer, did their comments bother me so much? Suddenly God's grace provided me with an answer. I was caught in this struggle because I wanted to rescue God, to protect God as I deemed necessary. Laughing to myself, I realized that it wasn't really necessary for me to take care of God in this way. In the healing quiet my spirit sensed "be still and know that I am God." Delighted and calmed, I ended my prayer, grateful for the humbling.

---

* Source: Teresa of Avila, *The Way of Perfection*, in *The Collected Works of St. Teresa of Avila* Vol. II, trans. Kieran Kavanaugh, OCD, and Otilio Rodriguez, OCD (Washington, DC: ICS Publications, 1980), chap. 39, 2, p. 189.

The Wow-isms of God

All who are free
tell me a thousand graceful things of you;
all wound me more
and leave me dying
of, ah, I-don't-know-what behind their stammering.
— John of the Cross*

The shepherds of the galaxies, the Hubble Telescope astronomers, have released photos of the universe from fourteen billion years ago. As I attempt to fathom the very notion of billions of years, my gaze settles on a large maple tree outdoors. Nestled in the fork of the trunk and a snow-covered limb, a squirrel wrapped in its tail is sleeping. Its ability to slumber while so precariously balanced is as mind boggling as the distance of light years – equally deserving of the "I-don't-know-what" of God.

Awareness is a gift. Meditation on God's mystery, whether it be the creation of the universe or the ingenuity of providing squirrels with tails for winter sleeping, is gift. The presence of God in one's life is a gift.

I came into relationship with the God of my present understanding only as a middle-aged adult. Therefore, I can completely relate to John of the Cross's struggle to articulate the great awesomeness of his God. I, too, "stammer" in attempting to comprehend God's miracles and mystery – indeed the WOW-ISMS of my God!

---

* Source: John of the Cross, *The Spiritual Canticle*, in *The Collected Works of St. John of the Cross*, trans. Kieran Kavanaugh, OCD, and Otilio Rodriguez, OCD rev. ed. (Washington, DC: ICS Publications, 1991), The Poem, Stanza 7, p. 472.

As Near As My Heart

How much more is it necessary not to withdraw
through one's own efforts from all our good and help
which is the most sacred humanity of our Lord Jesus
Christ.
— *Teresa of Avila*[*]

If asked to identify the most important reality in my life, I would, without hesitation, point to my relationship with Jesus Christ. Knowing that this God-become-human truly understands me is, for me, the most beautiful aspect of the Incarnation. It is the anchor of my life.

Over the years, I have struggled to accept the fact that Jesus truly loves me for who I am. Out of the struggle, I have come to a complete trust in his love, mercy, and forgiveness. At the same time, I have also come to know him as a true friend who gently challenges me in my journey toward wholeness.

My experience of Jesus is not as someone who lived two thousand years ago and then vanished into cosmic oblivion. Rather, he is someone who is as near to me as my own heart. It is only in relationship with him that I find true peace, joy, and a knowledge of my own personal worth.

---

[*]   Source: Teresa of Avila, *The Interior Castle*, in *The Collected Works of St. Teresa of Avila* Vol. II, trans. Kieran Kavanaugh, OCD, and Otilio Rodriguez, OCD (Washington, DC: ICS Publications, 1980), VI, chap. 7, 6, p. 399.

On Him Alone

*Fasten your eyes on [Christ] alone because in him I
have spoken and revealed all and in him you will
discover even more than you ask for and desire.*

— *John of the Cross*[*]

In today's world, there is an almost frantic search for
meaning and fulfillment. In the newspaper headlines or on the
television news we hear daily of murders, war, political and
corporate greed. Even the church is not immune, as there is
sometimes a tension between liberal and conservative, between
those who cherish reform and those who cherish tradition. We
can become frustrated and ask whether the person of Jesus
Christ, God with us, really makes a difference.

If we look only at the headlines and not beyond them, or
if we look only at the tragedies and not the triumphs (seeing
the deaths and not the resurrections), then we must say, no, the
One whom we recognize as Lord and Savior does not make a
difference in the world.

But if we say that we are believers in the One Sent,
professing that Jesus comes to liberate us from the worst of our
human condition, then our search for meaning and fulfillment
is over. To paraphrase a popular song, "The search is over. You
were with us all the while."

The Good News is that God's seal has been set upon Jesus
Christ. We must fasten our eyes on him alone, for in him God
has spoken and revealed all, and in him we will discover even
more than we ask for or desire.

---

[*] Source: John of the Cross, *The Ascent of Mount Carmel*, in *The Collected Works
of St. John of the Cross*, trans. Kieran Kavanaugh, OCD, and Otilio Rodriguez,
OCD (Washington, DC: ICS Publications, 1991) Book Two, chap. 22, 5, pp.
230-31.

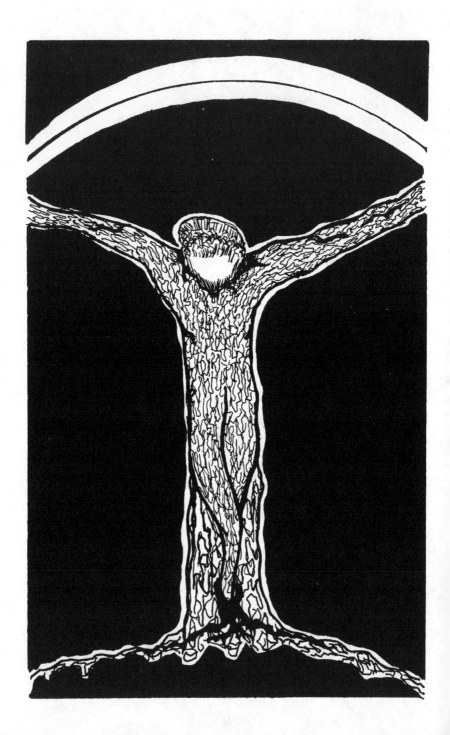

In the Midst of Suffering

*I will not ask God to deliver you from your trials, but
I will ask [God] earnestly to give you the patience and
strength needed to suffer as long as [God] desires.*

— *Brother Lawrence**

These words of Brother Lawrence raise many of the age-old questions regarding the mystery of human suffering. They are questions which have haunted me in both my personal and professional life.

In my personal life, I have little patience for suffering. Initially, I assume it must have been visited upon me by mistake. If it persists, however, I conclude that God must be sleeping on the job for surely there can be no redemptive value in prolonged affliction.

Or can there? Having worked in a hospital setting, I have seen the outcome go both ways. For some, suffering brings an embittered heart, a fatalistic sense of being scorned and abandoned. For others, suffering engenders compassion and humility.

Why are some destroyed while others find resurrection? The answer is undoubtedly complex. Experience, though, points to the forces of both nature and nurture. Some persons are just naturally more optimistic and hopeful than others. Others anticipate the worst and resign themselves to a type of living death.

Not all can be explained by reason, however, for in the midst of suffering we also find the element of grace. Against all odds, a soul grasps on to the power of God, and the strength and patience which Brother Lawrence refers to is achieved. A deep sense of serenity takes over, and we who observe it give thanks for the privilege of witnessing God's salvific hand at work.

---

* Source: Brother Lawrence (Nicolas Herman), *The Practice of the Presence of God*, trans. Salvatore Sciurba, OCD, (Washington, DC: ICS Publications, 1994) Letter 11, Nov. 17, 1690, p. 73.

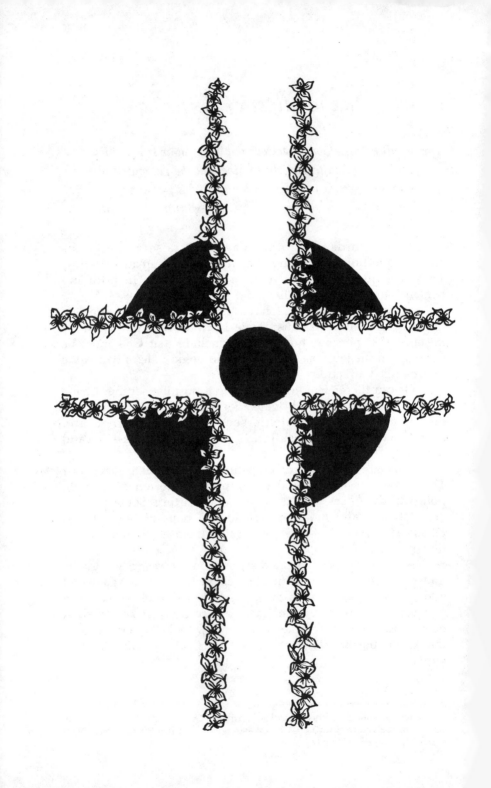

The Divine Embrace

*. . . I trust then in the mercy of God, who never fails
to repay anyone who has taken [God] for a friend. For
mental prayer . . . is nothing else then an intimate
sharing between friends; it means taking time
frequently to be alone with [the One] who we
know loves us.* — Teresa of Avila*

When are we comfortable with someone? Are we
comfortable with one who only makes us feel good but
abandons us when our world falls apart? Are we comfortable
with one who makes us feel powerful, but can't deal with our
frailty and weakness? No, I would say we are truly comfortable
with that true friend who cherishes us for who we truly are, at
every moment; when we feel we are living up to our ideal self
or when we are not.

In prayer, we know that we are with the One who loves
us unconditionally. If we truly believe in the Good News of
Jesus Christ, then we need no longer be afraid of our
weaknesses, our insecurities or even our sinfulness, because the
One whom Jesus teaches us to call Father/Mother embraces us
in total acceptance, total peace and total love.

* Source: Teresa of Avila, *The Book of Her Life*, in *The Collected Works of St.
Teresa of Avila* Vol. I, trans. Kieran Kavanaugh, OCD, and Otilio Rodriguez,
OCD rev. ed (Washington, DC: ICS Publications, 1987), chap. 8, 5, p. 96.

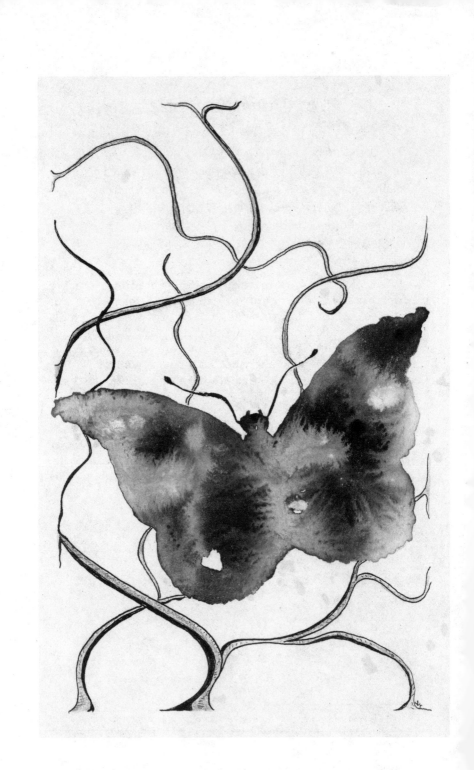

Now: Our Only Time for Loving

... I don't want to think of anything but the present
moment. — *Thérèse of Lisieux*[*]

St. Thérèse had a unique ability to see the integral relationship between reality and sanctity. Reality exists in the NOW, in the "eternity shut in a span." Perfection consists simply in doing and accepting God's will from moment to moment. Such moments are gifts, sent to deepen our love for God and one another. When grounded in faith and prayer, we find that each offers us a grace, whether it be in the form of joy, suffering, peace or dismay.

Unfortunately, many of us miss these graces. Instead, we look for heroic acts to present to God, ignoring the everyday opportunities for divine union. This is tragic because few of us will be called to outstanding moments of faith or love. Rather, we will be called to transcend the daily occurrences of hurt feelings, unpleasant neighbors, disappointments, and minor aches and pains.

Frequently we find this call to present day happiness challenging because we are more inclined to focus our energies on the past or in the future. However, the past is gone forever and the future may never be. All that we can be certain of is the NOW. NOW is the time to forget, to forgive and to heal. NOW is the time to fulfill our responsibilities, to give love and to share joy. As St. Thérèse reminds us, God's redemptive call is embedded in the immediacy of today.

---

[*] Source: Thérèse of Lisieux, *The "Yellow Notebook" of Mother Agnes*, in *ST. THÉRÈSE OF LISIEUX/Her Last Conversations*, trans. John Clarke, OCD, (Washington, DC: ICS Publications, 1977), August 23, #3, p. 165.

A Touching of God's Love

O gentle hand! O delicate touch that tastes of eternal
life. — *John of the Cross**

Pictured in his recent autobiography are Nelson Mandela and his great granddaughter. In the captured moment the baby is not at all impressed with this modern day giant whose life has exemplified such fidelity to justice and goodness. Rather, she is contented and delighted with a wonderful object directly within her sight and touch – President Mandela's nose! He in turn is radiantly accepting the child's touch – a touch of God's love.

How, I pray, might I more readily delight in each moment so that I too may radiate the touch of God's love?

---

* Source: John of the Cross, *The Living Flame of Love*, in *The Collected Works of St. John of the Cross*, trans. Kieran Kavanaugh, OCD, and Otilio Rodriguez, OCD rev. ed. (Washington, DC: ICS Publications, 1991) Stanza 2, p. 640.

Silent Listening

Pouring out a thousand graces,
he passed these groves in haste;
and having looked at them,
with his image alone,
clothed them in beauty.

— *John of the Cross**

No matter the method used to quiet the mind, at prayer most of us sometimes experience answers to questions popping up unexpectedly out of nowhere. The peaceful stance of prayer frees the mind to release what is needed for creative solutions. Educators tell us that all knowledge is within us, and that learning is a matter of freeing it up, letting it out.

Recently, after snagging just the word I needed for a crossword puzzle right in the middle of a morning meditation, I began to think about the unfolding of the mystery of God that is within each of us and within every thing. Is not the quieting role of prayer the readying of ourselves for that revelation?

Someone has said that the best way to pray is to let the mind settle as one would a muddy pond, allowing the treasures of the stream's bed to be revealed to us. But the revelation of God is not reserved solely for times of prayer. We can bring that gentle, respectful, silent listening to our encounters with one another and with every created thing. With an ever-prayerful approach, all creation can speak to us, everything can be a grace for us.

---

* Source: John of the Cross, *The Spiritual Canticle*, in *The Collected Works of St. John of the Cross*, trans. Kieran Kavanaugh, OCD, and Otilio Rodriguez, OCD rev. ed. (Washington, DC: ICS Publications, 1991), The Poem, stanza 5, p. 472.

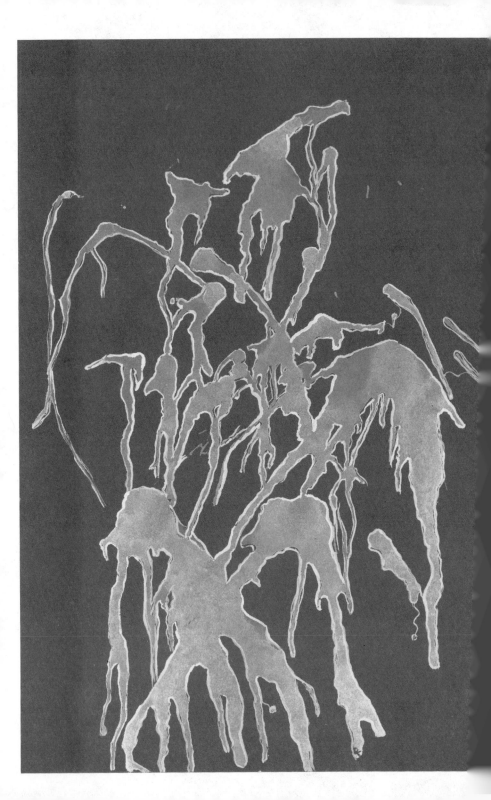

Thinning the Veil

O spring like crystal!
If only, on your silvered-over faces,
you would suddenly form
the eyes I have desired,
which I bear sketched deep within my heart.
                                    — *John of the Cross**

When his first son was about a year old, my brother, only half-jokingly, said of him: "The kid makes me nervous. He goes around acting as though he knows something I don't know." There is something about the freedom and trust of a loved child that speaks of the beyond. Children live an unabashed "I Am" that ignites a spark of wonder, if not envy, in the socialized adult. It is as though they have so recently been in touch with the initial act of creation that the veil between the divine and the human has not completely fallen into place.

Prayer, opening oneself to God, can thin the veil of the mystery of the Creator. This is not a return to the limitations of childhood, but a mature realization that we are totally dependent upon God who is consistently trustworthy and unconditionally loving.

For the poet all creation "silvers over" the Divine Presence. But he reminds us that a child-like approach to nature, to one another and to life, and a singlehearted search for and openness to God can ready us to experience breakthroughs of the Divine in everything and each event of our day-to-day lives.

Artists wait for hours for the right sunset or sunrise. Writers wait for the words to rise to their fingers. Pray-ers watch and wait for the revelation of God that is always mystery to their minds, but which they somehow recognize with their hearts. Children tell us much before they can talk. God also speaks without words.

---

* Source: John of the Cross, *The Spiritual Canticle*, in *The Collected Works of St. John of the Cross*, trans. Kieran Kavanaugh, OCD, and Otilio Rodriguez, OCD rev. ed. (Washington, DC: ICS Publications, 1991), The Poem, stanza 12, p. 473.

Turning in Trust

O Lord, how true that all harm comes to us from not keeping our eyes fixed on You.   — *Teresa of Avila**

In times of distress to "fix our eyes on God" is more than a matter of being distracted from what is unpleasant or painful. To imagine oneself before God is to open the way to another perception of an event or situation. From a human standpoint the event may have one appearance. In God's presence it may present a completely different source and possibility.

The negative experiences in our lives that show us how vulnerable and powerless we are can lure us to the realization of our real source of strength and courage. We believe that we come from God and that God's unconditional love sustains us; we believe that we will never be tried beyond our strength and that joy is a grace that God longs to bestow upon us. In times of stress we forget all this and begin to look to and depend upon our own resources.

When we are in need, the habit of turning to God, even when we are in doubt about God, is itself an act of faith. It is an act of love that we may not feel in our hearts. It is an attempt to attune ourselves to what is, and in that attempt we touch the truth and beauty and goodness that is God.

---

* Source: Teresa of Avila, *The Way of Perfection*, in *The Collected Works of St. Teresa of Avila* Vol. II, trans. Kieran Kavanaugh, OCD, and Otilio Rodriguez, OCD (Washington, DC: ICS Publications, 1980), chap. 16, 11, p. 97.

Stay with the Climb

Let nothing trouble you. . . . God alone suffices.

— *Teresa of Avila**

When my financial records for the year finally balanced, I jumped up and danced. It was about 10:30 in the evening, and I was so energized by the joy and freedom of the event that I kept doing small jobs for hours. I was especially aware of the feeling of freedom, for I needed to have the report out of the way to be able to do another job well. I kept thinking, "I'm free, I'm free."

When I finally reflected on what I was doing, I realized that I am always free. No matter how involved, tragic, embarrassing, rushed, or important a matter at hand might be, in the last analysis, I am free before God. If I do the best that I can – and even if I don't – God will continue to be God, a God who will never expect more of me than I can do or be.

In a society driven by workaholism, co-dependency, inferiority complexes, and competition, I find this experience of freedom life-giving. It speaks of the reality of our limitations and of God's blessings on them.

Our deepest source of joy and most powerful source of energy is our relationship with God, the life of God within. Teresa is not telling us to deny pain or to live a bland existence. She challenges the idolatry that lets us base our lives on passing joys and sorrows. Both are important stepping stones that lead us from their limited offerings to the limitless treasure that is union with God. Because they are so close to the human skin, they readily register their energy. In contrast, it takes perseverance and determination to stay with the climb of faith that keeps one going, even when the very nearness of God clouds or numbs all feeling. Teresa seems to be telling us that the goal is God, not God's gifts. Find freedom and courage in the life of faith.

---

* Source: Teresa of Avila, *Poetry*, in *The Collected Works of St. Teresa of Avila* Vol. III, trans. Kieran Kavanaugh, OCD, and Otilio Rodriguez, OCD (Washington, DC: ICS Publications, 1985), #9, Efficacy of Patience, p. 386.

Three Pillars

. . . love for one another . . . detachment . . . humility.
— *Teresa of Avila**.

These three directives of St. Teresa to her Carmelite daughters are helpful challenges for all of us who seek wholeness. The "spine" of these three Teresian pillars is reality. The core of humility is truth, detachment leads to freedom that is God's gift to us, and love for one another is the unifying force for peace and human living on this planet.

Teresa was guiding her sisters in a life of prayer which goes hand in hand with a life of virtue. Her goal was to open their minds and hearts to the Christlife within, and her life-plan is apt.

Humility frees the mind of pretense, allowing us to know the gift of who we are and who is calling us to union. Detachment releases the heart from the bondage of addiction and opens us to a longing for the ultimate good. Love for one another draws us out of ourselves, a kind of death that leads to life.

With this clean slate, so to speak, a person can be open to God in prayer and in life. We are creatures before our Creator, powerlessness before omnipotence, but more importantly, we are living embodiments of the Love that gives us life and calls us to realize our essential union with our Source.

---

* Source: Teresa of Avila, *The Way of Perfection*, in *The Collected Works of St. Teresa of Avila* Vol. II, trans. Kieran Kavanaugh, OCD, and Otilio Rodriguez, OCD (Washington, DC: ICS Publications, 1980), chap. 4, 4, p. 54.

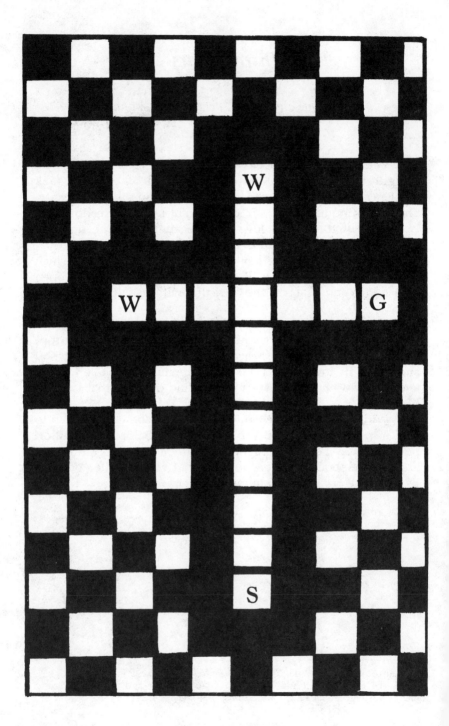

Completing the Puzzle

Oh, how desirable is this union with God's will!
— *Teresa of Avila**

Recently I found myself stumped on an entire corner of a crossword puzzle. I had confidently filled in **ranchtype** where it asked for "Like some houses," delighted to have come up with such a long word. I was sure of the first letter, and the word fit perfectly, but nothing around it seemed to connect.

A word that looked like it belonged in the block kept teasing me to try it, but it conflicted with **ranchtype**, to which I was becoming more and more attached. Finally I reluctantly erased **ranchtype** and wrote **in time** where the puzzle asked for "Eventually." Suddenly word after strange word popped out at me, and within about thirty seconds the entire corner of the puzzle came together.

I find this an apt analogy for what can happen in prayer. Often I go to God with a favorite "word" written in the stone of my willfulness. When I am willing to let God erase my plans and agendas – to let willingness replace willfulness – I come away from prayer with a new idea, God's word, and I am more together with God and myself than before I began.

---

* Source: Teresa of Avila, *The Interior Castle*, in *The Collected Works of St. Teresa of Avila* Vol. II, trans. Kieran Kavanaugh, OCD, and Otilio Rodriguez, OCD (Washington, DC: ICS Publications, 1980), V, chap. 3, 3, p. 349.

Is It a Sunny Day?

This is what we must strive for earnestly, to be affable,
agreeable, and pleasing to persons with whom we deal,
especially our Sisters. — *Teresa of Avila**

When one of my nephews began to talk, he used to greet his mother in the morning with, "Is it a sunny day?" That challenge from a sleepy-eyed toddler was surely enough to make his mother's day sunny no matter what the weather, and it also revealed that the child knew that sunny days can mean happy days. We know that too, and so did St. Teresa.

We all carry a bit of light and darkness within ourselves, and we have the freedom to shed one or the other on those around us. We know what it does to a group when someone with unrestrained gloom enters a room. We also know what a vibrant smile can do to a bus full of anxious commuters.

When St. Teresa tells her sisters to make it easy for others to like them, she is not suggesting that they engage in a popularity contest. Getting along with others is not always easy, and Teresa is giving her readers a genuine way of lightening the burden.

This is not an invitation to deny one's feelings of sorrow or to produce a Pollyanna countenance. It is a challenge to use one's freedom to place the good of others before oneself. The bottom line here is charity. We may not be able to make peace happen in a war-torn country or stem the tide of violence on our streets. But in our own homes, offices, or communities we have the power to make it a little easier for gentleness and peace and sometimes joy to be the abiding atmosphere.

---

* Source: Teresa of Avila, *The Way of Perfection*, in *The Collected Works of St. Teresa of Avila* Vol. II, trans. Kieran Kavanaugh, OCD, and Otilio Rodriguez, OCD (Washington, DC: ICS Publications, 1980), chap. 41, 7, p. 200.

Bearing Love's Power

For are there persons who can be so like brutes that
they will not love each other even though they must
always deal with and be in the company of one
another . . . and believe that God loves them and
they [God] . . . ? — Teresa of Avila[*]

It is usually not too difficult to overlook the faults of those we love. At the same time, Teresa's words are a challenge, for there comes a time when in the daily grind, we find ourselves chafing at the idiosyncrasies of those nearest and dearest to us.

It is only recently that I have discovered why I have always been drawn to this challenge. Isn't this reminder to love the neighbor who is near – and perhaps known too well – merely a microcosm of the gospel's universal call to love, forgiveness and compassion? We all long to do something about the conflicts that devastate the world. Can this be a way for us?

At the Last Supper Jesus prayed that we all may be one. In fact we are one, and the challenge for us is to realize our unity and our connectedness, to realize that everything we do affects the entire world. My move to understand, to forgive and be compassionate toward another who annoys me can mobilize to mercy a soldier who is thousands of miles away. It can inspire mediation among world leaders. At any moment I can pour into the world either love or hate energy. I can build or I can destroy. We are born of God's love, and we bear the power of that love.

[*] Source: Teresa of Avila, *The Way of Perfection,* in *The Collected Works of St. Teresa of Avila* Vol. II, trans. Kieran Kavanaugh, OCD, and Otilio Rodriguez, OCD (Washington, DC: ICS Publications, 1980), chap. 4, 10, p. 56.

Anyone in Need

Do you want to be totally united to the Crucified? If you are serious about this, you will be present, by the power of his Cross, at every front, at every place of sorrow, bringing to those who suffer comfort, healing, and salvation.
— Edith Stein[*]

Sister Teresa Benedicta of the Cross, (Edith Stein,) left the above jottings in her unpublished papers in the monastery in Cologne, Germany. Considering her exemplary charity during her internment in the Nazi prison camps before her execution, one could be tempted to think that she had come to this insight in the leveling experience of utter powerlessness and desperate suffering. Rather, the more ordinary experiences of life had inched her toward this realization, a realization which both prepared her for what was to come and enabled her to live out her belief.

Edith believed that the Holy Spirit is alive in every person, waiting like a tender bud, ready to open and reveal itself at the least breath of interest and willingness on our part. She had developed the quiet art of listening for and to that Spirit within, and this enabled her to begin to see as God sees. God, who in Christ sees the Christ-life in all, sees every person as child, anointed and beloved.

Quiet listening to the whisperings of the truth within can lead us to a spirit of solidarity with the neighbor in need, calling us to creative collaboration for the good of all. As we reach for Edith Stein's degree of perception, perhaps the "neighbor" whom we must first welcome is the Spirit of God within us. Only then will we be able to move beyond a patronizing stance and reach out to others with the limitless charity of Christ.

---

[*] Source: Edith Stein, Sister Teresa Benedicta of the Cross, *Life in a Jewish Family,*in *The Collected Works of Edith Stein* Vol. I, trans. Josephine Koeppel, OCD (Washington, DC: ICS Publications, 1986), Chronology, p. 435.

Love Alone

I understood that LOVE COMPRISED ALL
VOCATIONS, THAT LOVE WAS EVERYTHING,
THAT IT EMBRACED ALL TIMES AND PLACES.
. . . IN A WORD, THAT IT WAS ETERNAL! . . .
my vocation, at last I have found it. . . .
MY VOCATION IS LOVE!   — *Thérèse of Lisieux*[*]

Thérèse reminds us that wherever we are and whatever we do, our vital and eternal vocation is love. God invites us to bring love into our lives every single moment and to extend that love to those we touch each day. Our God is a family God, three Divine Persons in love with each other and with all of their needy children. We must daily savor this priceless truth and abide in this love.

Gandhi hinted at the breadth of God's love when he said, "If you don't find God in the very next person you meet, it is a waste of time to look any further." Thérèse understood this holy wisdom. Love was the only word beneath her pen, on her lips and in her heart. She wrote, "One sole desire makes my heart beat and it is the love I shall receive and the love I shall be able to give."

Thérèse's powerlessness was the very cause of her joy because she knew that God responds to the needy, the empty, the cry of the poor. She knew that the more God wishes to give us, the more God makes us desire. Jesus taught her to do everything for love and to refuse God nothing, and in proving her love for God and for others, she was gifted with gratitude, happiness and peace.

---

[*] Source: Thérèse of Lisieux, *Manuscript B*, in *STORY OF A SOUL/The Autobiography of St. Thérèse of Lisieux*, trans. John Clarke, OCD (Washington, DC: ICS Publications, 1975), chap. 9, p. 194.

Oklahoma City

The shepherd says: I pity the one
who draws herself back from my love,
and does not seek the joy of my presence,
though my heart is an open wound with love for her.
                              — *John of the Cross**

Violence is a contagious dis-ease that infiltrates the lives of those who contact it in any way. After the initial paralysis of the shock of it subsides, it is a rare person who does not experience the symptoms of anger, hate, or revenge. The victim or witness is breathing the air of a foreign, contaminated atmosphere. The wounded person momentarily experiences a loss of equilibrium.

Violence generates an energy that urges action, and it is vital to realize that one has the freedom to choose how to use that energy. To return to the stability of one's true self, violence must be flushed out of the system, and the person needs to be returned to a former healthy space. This, too, calls for action, an action that can employ the energy of the very violence that necessitates it. But how can anyone call forth this free choice at such a stressful time?

Everyone contains a survival back-up of spiritual gifts of charity, joy, peace, patience, mildness, and more – the healing "white cells" of the soul. This inner power can be released, despite the anger, tension, and horror one feels.

Surrendering to violence and revenge leads to the death of the moral person that the victim once was. The desire to choose life is the catalyst that moves a victim to positive action. By deliberately choosing to pray for the offender, by reaching out to others in acts of goodness that engage and change one's thoughts to thoughts of love and peace – by such responses – one clears the air of violence and turns in the direction of healing and former well-being.

---

* Source: John of the Cross, *The Poetry*, in *The Collected Works of St. John of the Cross*, trans. Kieran Kavanaugh, OCD, and Otilio Rodriguez, OCD rev. ed. (Washington, DC: ICS Publications, 1991), Poem #7, stanza 4, p. 58.

Violence crucifies us all, but every time someone responds with love and forgiveness, that person and all humankind are raised up to a new vision and quality of life. This is salvation. This is mirroring the God who makes good come of evil. This is the beginning of the end of violence.